STECK-VAUGHN
PORTRAIT OF AMERICA

Idaho

Steck-Vaughn Company

Executive Editor	Diane Sharpe
Senior Editor	Martin S. Saiewitz
Design Manager	Pamela Heaney
Photo Editor	Margie Foster
Electronic Cover Graphics	Alan Klemp

Proof Positive/Farrowlyne Associates, Inc.
Program Editorial, Revision Development, Design, and Production

Consultant: Judith Austin, Coordinator of Publications, Idaho State Historical Society

Published by Raintree Steck-Vaughn Publishers, an imprint of Steck-Vaughn Company.

A Turner Educational Services, Inc. book. Based on the Portrait of America television series by R. E. (Ted) Turner.

Cover Photo: Cover photography of Ann Morrison Park, Boise by © Gerald French/FPG.

Library of Congress Cataloging-in-Publication Data

Thompson, Kathleen.
    Idaho / Kathleen Thompson.
        p. cm. — (Portrait of America)
    "Based on the Portrait of America television series"—T.p. verso.
    "A Turner book."
    Includes index.
    ISBN 0-8114-7332-5 (library binding).—ISBN 0-8114-7437-2 (softcover)
    1. Idaho—Juvenile literature. [1. Idaho.] I. Title. II. Series:
Thompson, Kathleen. Portrait of America.
F746.3.T45 1996
979.6—dc20
                                    95-25731
                                      CIP
                                      AC

Printed and Bound in the United States of America

3 4 5 6 7 8 9 10 WZ 03 02 01 00 99

Acknowledgments
The publishers wish to thank the following for permission to reproduce photographs:
P. 7 © Gary Brettnacher/Tony Stone Images; p. 8 Nez Perce National Historic Park, National Park Service; pp. 10, 11 Idaho State Historical Society; p. 13 © Chris Chaffin/U.S. Forest Service; p. 14 (top) Idaho State Historical Society, (bottom) Idaho Department of Parks & Recreation; p. 15 (both), 16 Idaho State Historical Society; p. 17 (top) Boise Convention & Visitors Bureau, (bottom) Idaho State Historical Society; p. 18 Idaho State Historical Society; p. 19 (top) Idaho State Historical Society, (bottom) Idaho Power Company; pp. 20, 21, 23 Idaho State Historical Society; pp. 24, 25 Nez Perce National Historic Park, National Park Service; p. 26 © Mark Gibson/Southern Stock; p. 28 Wool Growers' Association; p. 29 (top) © Heather Paul, Moscow, ID, Idaho Wheat Commission, (bottom) © Pam Benham Photography, Hailey, ID, Idaho Wheat Commission; p. 30 Boise Cascade Corporation; p. 31 © Andrew Kent/Sun Valley Company; pp. 32, 33 © David H. Archibald, Potato Growers of Idaho Magazine, Harris Publishing Inc.; p. 34 Idaho State Historical Society; p. 35 (left) © David H. Archibald, Potato Growers of Idaho Magazine, Harris Publishing Inc., (right) Ore-Ida Foods, Inc.; p. 36 © Scott Melcer; p. 38 (both) Idaho Department of Parks & Recreation; p. 39 (top) Sun Valley Company, (bottom) Nez Perce National Historic Park, National Park Service; p. 40 Courtesy Susan Kennedy; p. 41 (top) Courtesy Mary Blackstock, (bottom) Courtesy Susan Kennedy; p. 42 © Steve Bly/Tony Stone Images; p. 44 Hewlett-Packard; p. 46 One Mile Up; p. 47 (left) One Mile Up, (center) © William D. Bransford/National Wildflower Research Center, (right) © Anthony Mercieca/Photo Researchers.

STECK-VAUGHN
PORTRAIT OF AMERICA

Idaho

Kathleen Thompson

A Turner Book

RSVP
RAINTREE
STECK-VAUGHN
PUBLISHERS
The Steck-Vaughn Company

Austin, Texas

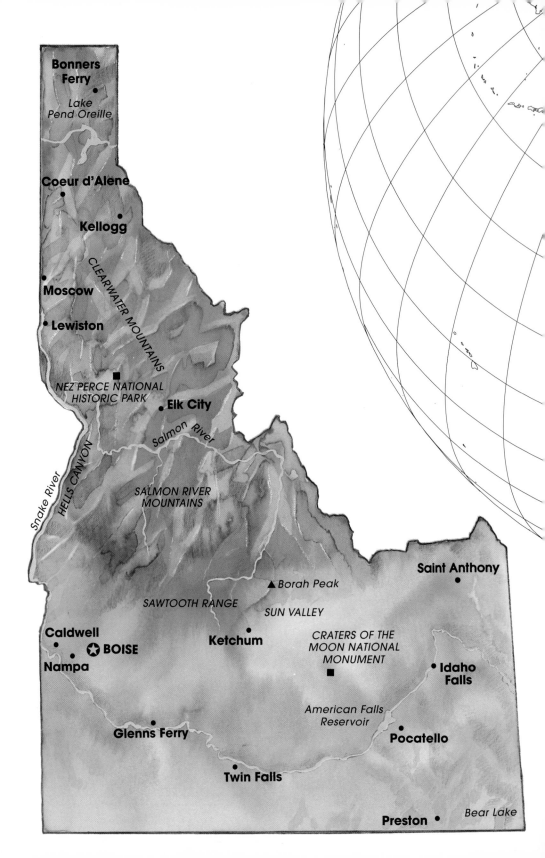

Idaho

Bonners
Ferry
Lake
Pend Oreille
Coeur d'Alene
Kellogg
CLEARWATER MOUNTAINS
Moscow
Lewiston
NEZ PERCE NATIONAL
HISTORIC PARK
Elk City
Salmon River
Snake River
HELLS CANYON
SALMON RIVER
MOUNTAINS
Saint Anthony
Borah Peak
SAWTOOTH RANGE
SUN VALLEY
Caldwell
BOISE
Ketchum
CRATERS OF THE
MOON NATIONAL
MONUMENT
Idaho
Falls
Nampa
American Falls
Reservoir
Glenns Ferry
Pocatello
Twin Falls
Preston
Bear Lake

Contents

Introduction

If you get someone from Idaho to tell you about their state, they'll probably use words such as *deepest*, *longest*, and *highest*. They won't be just bragging. Idaho, a Rocky Mountain state, deserves these descriptions. Hells Canyon, at 7,900 feet, is the deepest canyon in North America. The Salmon River is the longest river to lie entirely within one state's boundaries. Shoshone Falls is one of the highest waterfalls in the world. The drop from these falls is farther than that of Niagara Falls. People from Idaho will no doubt use the word *most*, too. The state raises the most potatoes in the United States, and it has some of the most rugged mountains in the Northwest—the Bighorn Crags. It also boasts one of the most beautiful lakes in the world, Coeur d'Alene Lake. Idaho is a state that has a little of everything.

Alpine mountain skiing is only one of the many winter activities that can be enjoyed in Idaho. Others include snowboarding, snowmobiling, sled-dog racing, and cross-country skiing.

Idaho

The Freedom of Open Land

Long after much of the rest of the United States was settled, the area we now call Idaho remained a wilderness. Native American groups called Nez Perce, Kutenai, Pend d'Oreille, and Coeur d'Alene lived in the northern region. The Bannock, also known as the Paiute, and the Shoshone lived in the southern portion. These groups raised horses that enabled them to hunt buffalo, which migrated through the Great Plains. They also hunted game, fished in the rivers and streams, and gathered wild plants, seeds, and nuts. Much of what the land offered, the Native Americans found useful.

In 1803 the United States purchased a huge area of land that had been claimed by France. The land included the entire Mississippi River basin from New Orleans to the Canadian border and west to the Rocky Mountains. This land deal, known as the Louisiana Purchase, doubled the size of the United States. In 1803 President Thomas Jefferson sent Meriwether Lewis and William Clark to explore the new land for

This traditional Nez Perce bag is an artifact of a civilization that has lived in Idaho for thousands of years.

a route to the Pacific Ocean. Lewis and Clark's expedition established a route that opened up the West to others. The explorers charted the Salmon and Clearwater country in north-central Idaho in 1805.

Fur trappers first began arriving in present-day Idaho in 1809. British and French trappers competed with trappers from the United States for beaver furs in the Snake River area. The trappers came in greater numbers after 1824 as the fur trade became established. They set up trading posts in the area and traded with the Native Americans, exchanging cloth, knives, and cooking utensils for furs.

Missionaries began arriving in the area by 1836 and continued throughout the 1840s. Their purpose was to convert Native Americans to Christianity. Presbyterian minister Henry Spalding and his wife, Eliza, were among the first settlers of European descent in the Idaho region. They established the Lapwai Mission near present-day Lewiston. They also built the first sawmill, the first flour mill, the first church, the first school, and had the first printing press there.

Another religious group, the Mormons, arrived in eastern Idaho in 1855. The Mormons wanted to start a colony in the West after enduring religious persecution for some of their religious beliefs. Most of them eventually ended up in present-day Utah, but some were sent to colonize areas farther north in Idaho. Mormon settlers cut down trees and cleared the land for farming. They plowed and cultivated the land and even irrigated it. The Mormons got along with the Native Americans, but they increasingly found themselves

Reverend Henry Spalding was the first European settler in Idaho, but he didn't stay. After 11 years, he moved to Oregon.

Early settlers in Idaho farmed the land using crude, horse-drawn machinery.

caught in the middle of battles between the Bannock and the Nez Perce. They left after Native Americans attacked their settlement in 1858. Another group of Mormons moved northward from Utah in 1860. They established the town of Franklin, in the far southeastern corner of the state. This became the region's first permanent settlement.

That same year, gold was discovered near Orofino Creek in north-central Idaho. During the next two years, prospectors stampeded into the area. Goldfields were opened near Elk City and Florence, as well as farther south in the Boise Basin. Mines also were dug along the Salmon River in central Idaho. The gold rush was on.

At that time Idaho was part of the Washington Territory, which extended east from Puget Sound to the continental divide. A majority of the territory's population lived in present-day Idaho. In 1863 there were about seventy thousand people in the Washington Territory. The people who ran the territorial government at Olympia felt the eastern part of the territory had too many people. They urged the United States Congress to make Idaho a separate territory. On March 4, 1863, the new Idaho Territory was established by Congress with Lewiston as its capital. The capital was moved to Boise a year later, as Idaho's population shifted south.

The Idaho Territory was huge. It included all of present-day Montana and most of what is now Wyoming. Gold miners were only the first wave of settlers to come into the Idaho Territory. They were followed by ranchers and farmers who came to raise food for the growing population of settlers.

Most booms go bust before too long. By 1870, only ten years after the first discovery of gold in Idaho Territory, only about 15,000 people still lived in the territory. When the gold ran out, many of the miners left to look elsewhere. Others stayed and worked in the newly established silver and lead mines near Hailey. The Coeur d'Alene mines in the north opened in the 1880s. Farmers and ranchers who stayed were joined by others arriving by the Oregon Short Line Railroad and the wagon caravans from Utah.

To make room for settlers, the United States government made many land treaties with the Native Americans. These treaties usually stated that if the Native Americans would move, they would be guaranteed a place to live elsewhere. Sometimes the government promised to pay the Native Americans. But the Native Americans had very little choice in the matter. The settlers were moving onto the land anyway. The Native Americans felt that it would be better to accept a guarantee of some land than to lose it all.

As more and more settlers arrived in the 1870s, the federal government broke its own treaties and demanded that the Native Americans accept even smaller portions of land. Often these were barren spots that no settlers wanted. In 1877 the United States Army forced the Nez Perce to accept a reservation in western Idaho. Some members of the Nez Perce attacked settlers nearby, which started a confrontation with federal troops. Chief Joseph led the Nez Perce into battle and gained a victory over the army at White Bird Canyon in central Idaho. Joseph was determined to flee to Canada rather than continue fighting against so many troops. After more than three months of running and fighting, the Nez Perce were surrounded and forced to surrender.

Another conflict over a broken treaty occurred in 1878 between the government and the Bannock. For 12 years the Bannock had lived at the Fort Hall Reservation in southern Idaho. Their treaty with the United States government was violated when Bannock lands were opened to settlers whose cattle ate prairie plants the

Moose are only one of many animals that roam Idaho's vast wilderness areas.

Many union members were imprisoned during the Idaho mining wars of the 1890s. Here, some of the prisoners exercise while carrying wooden rifles.

Bannock used for food. The Bannock, led by Chief Buffalo Horn, left the reservation, and a series of clashes took place between the Bannocks and settlers. Cattle ranchers became alarmed and called for federal troops. Chief Buffalo Horn and a number of Bannocks were killed in the battles that followed.

In 1889 Idaho's citizens adopted a state constitution, which was required for a territory to become a state. On July 3, 1890, Idaho became the forty-third state.

The battles with the Native Americans were mostly over, but the new state was not at peace. During the 1890s, miners protested the working conditions in the lead and silver mines of the Coeur d'Alene mining district in northern Idaho. Some of them joined labor unions, groups that demanded fairer treatment from the mine owners. Conflicts between the miners and the owners over wages broke out in 1892 at the Coeur d'Alene mining district. In 1899 skirmishes developed

Pioneers traveling the Oregon Trail sometimes carved their names in rock when they stopped to rest.

again, and Governor Frank Steunenberg called for federal troops to keep order.

Idaho changed politically in the late 1890s. In 1896 an amendment to the state constitution gave women the right to vote. Idaho was one of the first states to have female voters. The people of the state also grew concerned about preserving the state's wildlife areas. They asked the United States Congress to set aside some land as protected national forests. The state also passed laws to regulate hunting and fishing. Fire patrols were created to protect the timberlands. In 1905 and 1906, irrigation projects using water from the Snake River created more farmland.

Idaho developed rapidly in the early 1900s, spurred by a growing lumber industry. Farm and forest products were marketed across the nation. Large-scale mining developed in all parts of the state. The entry of the United States into

Idaho rivers really do grow large fish! The sturgeon in this 1908 photograph was caught in a deep pool of the Snake River. It weighed 632 pounds and measured 10 feet, 11 inches long.

With parasols raised against the summer sun, Idaho women march in support of their right to vote during the 1880s.

15

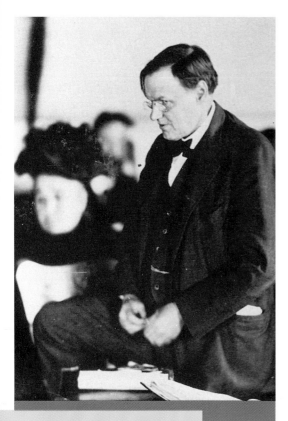

Clarence Darrow, the most famous attorney of his time, defended three union leaders accused of the 1905 murder of Idaho's former governor. Here, Darrow stands in the courtroom to make a point.

World War I in 1917 brought further prosperity to Idaho farmers. But, as with many other farm states, the war began a cycle of good and bad times that continued for many years. Because of wartime food shortages, prices were high. Farmers borrowed money to expand. With more land under cultivation, farmers made a good profit. But when the war ended, food prices plunged because the need for the crops went down. The farmers couldn't keep up the payments on their added acreage. While many industrial centers in the northern and eastern states were booming in the 1920s, low food prices kept Idaho and some other farm states in trouble.

In the 1930s the Great Depression hit the country. Many companies went out of business, and hundreds of thousands of people were out of work. The 1930s were also a time when many of the farm states southeast of Idaho were devastated by a major drought. For several years in a row, the farm states on the Great Plains had very little rainfall. The soil dried up, and strong winds swept it away. The area became known as the Dust Bowl. Many of the farmers simply abandoned their land and looked for someplace better to farm. Many traveled west to California. Others moved north to Idaho, where the drought had not spread. Federal loans helped the new residents buy farms.

The United States became involved in World War II on December 7, 1941, when Japanese forces bombed

Pearl Harbor, a United States Navy base in Hawaii. Important military bases were built in Idaho, including a large naval training station on Lake Pend Oreille, air bases at Boise, Pocatello, and Mountain Home, and a naval gun plant at Pocatello. In 1942 the federal government rounded up about 110,000 Japanese Americans from the West Coast and sent them to internment camps. About ten thousand Japanese Americans were interned at Camp Minidoka in south-central Idaho. The federal government was concerned that the Japanese Americans might try to help Japan's military forces fight against the United States. Many Japanese Americans lost their homes and possessions while they were detained in the camps. When they finally were released in 1945, many stayed in Idaho.

Idaho's lumber industry profited from a nationwide housing boom after the war ended in 1945. In 1949 the United States Atomic Energy Commission located some of its research sites in Idaho. A National Reactor

Many Idaho farmers lost their farms during the Great Depression of the 1930s. Abandoned buildings and corrals like these still dot the remote areas of the state.

Japanese Americans from the West Coast were relocated to internment camps despite the fact that those who were considered risks to the government had already been arrested.

Testing Station was built west of Idaho Falls in the southeastern part of the state. Two years later nuclear energy was used in the area to generate electricity for the very first time. In 1955 a one-hour test at that site revealed that one nuclear reactor could generate enough power for an entire community.

During the late 1950s and the 1960s, Idaho's population gradually became more urban. As with many farm states, improved farming methods and machinery meant that fewer people were needed to work the farms. By 1960 half the population of Idaho lived in cities or towns, where most of the jobs were located. Manufacturing replaced farming as the state's most important industry. Tourism was growing rapidly. People from other states were discovering Idaho's wilderness beauty. Sun Valley, in central Idaho, was one of the first major ski resorts in the western states. It was established in the 1930s.

In recent years Idaho has suffered several disasters. An underground fire broke out in the Sunshine Silver Mine in Shoshone County in 1972. Before it could be brought under control, the fire claimed 91 lives. Then, in 1976 the Teton Dam in southeastern Idaho

In 1955 this nuclear power facility, near Arco in southeastern Idaho, was the first to produce electric power for an entire town.

collapsed. Billions of gallons of water roared through farming communities downstream from the dam. Eleven people drowned. Damage to property totaled at least four hundred million dollars. In 1988 a drought destroyed Idaho's harvest and caused forest fires.

Today, one of the most important issues facing Idaho is the preservation of its wilderness. Idaho has more protected wilderness areas than any other state except Alaska. But its factories need water and electrical power. So owners of industrial companies want more dams built along the Snake River. This huge river runs along the state's western border, then curves eastward across the lower part of the state. The Idaho Power Company built three dams along the Snake River between 1959 and 1968. There are other dams along the Snake River, also. Some people think there should be more dams, while others argue against any further development.

While much of the United States was being settled, Idaho's wilderness was protected because it was so far from the growing population. Today, modern transportation means it is no longer isolated. Its scenic beauty and undeveloped landscapes are protected mainly by the people who love the land and call it home.

The Teton Dam collapsed in 1976, resulting in massive flooding all along the Upper Snake River valley.

This is one of the Snake River dams built by the Idaho Power Company in the 1950s.

Across the Oregon Trail

All along the two thousand miles of the Oregon Trail, westbound pioneers sang to keep their spirits up. They sang songs like the following:

"They're coming up the hill,
And my heart is standing still,
And we probably won't be here
    come the morning."

Wherever they were, they probably *wouldn't* be there the next morning. They had, at most, six months of warm weather to make the trek. They had to average at least 12 miles a day, so they needed to keep moving.

Idaho is one of the western states that counts the Oregon Trail as an important part of its heritage. In 1993, along with other states, Idaho celebrated the 150th anniversary of the trail's opening.

The Oregon Trail originated in Independence, Missouri. From there it wound westward, crossing parts of Kansas, Nebraska, Wyoming, Idaho, and Oregon. For much of its route, the trail followed rivers, which provided

Even as late as 1900, parts of the Oregon Trail were still used. This photo shows wagons hauling hay.

In 1900 Idaho City was still a frontier town with unpaved streets.

plenty of water and good grazing for the livestock. River valleys often were flat and were the least difficult way through the mountains. Large parts of the four-hundred-mile trail in Idaho followed the Bear and Snake rivers.

At Fort Hall, an old fur-trading post in southeastern Idaho, pioneers had to make a hard decision. They could follow the main trail along the Snake River, or they could strike off straight west, joining the Snake River in western Idaho. The second route was shorter and could reduce the journey by several weeks. But in those days, southern Idaho was a forbidding desert. Many cattle and oxen, and quite a few pioneers, lost their lives trying the shorter route. A third route branched off and headed southwest to California. Most of the pioneers kept on for Oregon, however, where free farmland was available for settlers.

Between 1843 and 1880, perhaps as many as fifty thousand pioneers followed the Oregon Trail. Often they had little idea what lay before them when they started out. All of them believed that they would find a better life at the end of the trail. Most of them went right on through Idaho. They were looking for the promised land, and they didn't see it in the sagebrush desert. When gold was discovered in Idaho, some of them returned.

In some places in Idaho, there are still ruts worn in the trail by thousands of wagons. Those ruts bore the burden of the pioneers, their precious belongings, and their hopes and dreams of a better life ahead.

Chief Joseph of the Nez Perce

Chief Joseph was a man of peace who had never set out to become one of history's great war chiefs. As a leader of the Nez Perce, Joseph watched as settlers advanced on his people's homeland. Although the Nez Perce endured broken treaties and fought many battles, Joseph's desire for peace never wavered. All he asked for himself and his people were the basic rights he believed were due to all people. He tried to obtain these rights for the Nez Perce until the end of his life.

Joseph's Native American name was In-mut-too-yah-lat-lat, which means "thunder rolling in the mountains." Joseph was born in 1840, the son of a leader also named Joseph. At that time settlers, trappers, and traders had already begun moving into Nez Perce lands in central Idaho and Oregon. In fact when he was a child, Joseph attended a nearby missionary school where he learned to speak English. He and his family, however, continued to hunt buffalo, raise horses, and practice their traditional religion.

In 1855 the Nez Perce signed a treaty with the United States government. The treaty stated that the Nez Perce would be given a large piece of land on which to live. However, the treaty also stated that the Nez Perce must stay on the land because settlers would own the surrounding land. The Nez Perce agreed, since the land stated in the treaty included much of their traditional territory.

In 1860 gold was discovered on Nez Perce land. Three years later the United States government rewrote the original treaty and reduced the size of Nez Perce territory from ten thousand square miles to one thousand square miles. The Nez Perce were allowed to live only on a small stretch of land in Oregon's Wallowa Valley. Many of the Nez Perce were angry about the treaty.

When his father died in 1871, Joseph became chief of the Nez Perce of the Wallowa Valley. Chief Joseph tried to stay at peace with the settlers, but in 1877 the federal government demanded that the Nez Perce move once again, this time to the Lapwai Reservation in Idaho. Joseph argued

Chief Joseph surrendered in order to save the lives of those who followed him.

chance to save his people. The Nez Perce would have to cover a distance of more than one thousand miles.

Joseph and over two hundred men and their families set out for Canada. The United States Army troops were never very far behind. Over the course of three and a half months, Joseph and the Nez Perce were pursued by the soldiers through most of Idaho and Montana. Every time the soldiers got too close, the Nez Perce fought so they could gain some distance again. Joseph led his people over mountains and through forests that had no paths. They rarely took much time to rest. The Nez Perce became weary of fighting and running. Many of the men had been killed. Those who were left were mostly women, children, and old people. Still the soldiers kept coming.

Government troops surrounded the Nez Perce camp when they were only 30 miles away from the Canadian border. There was no way out. Joseph rode out to meet with Colonel Nelson A. Miles and handed over his rifle. He is reported to have said, ". . . I am tired of fighting. Our chiefs are killed. . . . It is cold and we have no blankets. The

against this forced move. In the end, however, he agreed to leave peacefully. As he and his people were preparing to go, some Nez Perce warriors killed more than a dozen settlers. When Joseph learned of this incident, he knew the soldiers would come for his people. He came up with a daring plan to take the Nez Perce north to Canada. Joseph knew it would be a hard journey, but he believed it was the only

little children are freezing. We have no food. Hear me, my chiefs. I am tired. My heart is sick and sad. From where the sun now stands, I will fight no more forever."

The government promised to let the Nez Perce stay in Idaho. Instead they were sent to a reservation in Kansas, then to another in Oklahoma. Finally they were sent to a reservation in Washington. In 1879 Joseph addressed a large gathering of government officials and members of the United States Congress. He appealed to them to allow the Nez Perce to return to their original territory. During the meeting Joseph said these words: "I have shaken hands with a great many friends, but there are some things I want to know which no one seems able to explain. I cannot understand how the government sends a man out to fight us, as it did General Miles, and then breaks his word. Such a government has something wrong about it. . . .

"I only ask of the government to be treated as all other men are treated.

On July 4, 1898, Nez Perce, Lapwai, and Umatilla gathered at Lapwai for a celebration.

If I cannot go to my own home, let me have a home in a country where my people will not die so fast. . . . Let me be a free man—free to travel, free to stop, free to work, free to trade where I choose, free to choose my own teachers, free to follow the religion of my fathers, free to think and talk and act for myself—and I will obey every law or submit to penalty."

In 1885 the federal government allowed a small group of Nez Perce women and children to return to the Wallowa Valley. Joseph, however, was not allowed to accompany them. He spent the rest of his life on the Washington reservation and died on September 21, 1904.

This 1906 photograph shows a group of Nez Perce.

Relying on Resources

Like many other western states, Idaho's economy has gone through several major changes since it was settled. Idaho's early focus was on fur trading and mining. Later, the state relied more heavily on lumbering and agriculture. Today, the emphasis is on manufacturing and service industries. Idaho has undergone all these changes in a period of about a century and a half.

Water has been called the state's greatest resource. It is used for generating electricity and for irrigating land that otherwise would not support agriculture. Idaho has five major river systems, more than almost all other states. Its largest is the Snake River, which flows from east to west across southern Idaho, then turns north to form part of the state's western boundary. Massive irrigation projects that tap the waters of the Snake River have brought farming to this region. Today, southern Idaho is where most of the farming takes place. The state's river systems also provide abundant hydroelectric, or water-generated electrical power.

Federal and state agencies provide much of the employment in Boise, Idaho's capital and largest city. Pictured here is the water fountain in front of Boise's City Hall.

Sheep graze in the highlands where the grass is not good enough for cattle. Idaho is a leading producer of wool and lamb meat.

Dams and generators have been built on several rivers, providing the entire state with low-cost electricity.

Idaho's agriculture industry can be subdivided into two major categories: farming and ranching. Crop production is Idaho's biggest income-producer in this category. The three most important crops grown in the state are potatoes, wheat, and hay.

Potatoes are grown in the irrigated lands of the Snake River area. Idaho is the leading potato producer in the country. About one-third of all potatoes grown in the United States come from this region. Idaho is identified with the potato as much as Florida is with the orange or Georgia with the peach.

The same area in the Snake River basin where potatoes are grown also produces wheat. Hay, which is used mostly to feed grazing animals, is grown throughout Idaho. The state also is one of the nation's leading barley producers. Sugar beets are another important Idaho crop. In addition fruits and vegetables are grown in the southwestern region.

In the ranching category, beef cattle are Idaho's leading livestock. Beef cattle are raised strictly for their meat value. These animals graze on the range from the southern part of the state north to the central mountains. In the southern part of this region, dairy cattle also are raised. On some of the land where the grazing does not contain the nutrients necessary for beef cattle or dairy cows, ranchers raise sheep for meat and wool.

Though Idaho is more famous for potatoes, many of its farmers also grow wheat.

Manufacturing contributes about 18 percent of the gross state product, which is composed of all goods and services produced in the state. Agriculture contributes about 9 percent. Most of the manufacturing in Idaho is linked to the state's natural resources. The two most valuable industries are food processing and chemical manufacturing.

Food processing is the state's number one manufacturing industry. Just as you might expect in a state that raises so many potatoes, getting them ready for market is an important industry. Idaho has about twenty potato-processing plants. Some of these factories wash and package the potatoes. Others take on more complicated tasks, such as peeling, cutting, and dehydrating them into an endless variety of french fries, hash browns, potato puffs and patties, and instant mashed potatoes.

Idaho grain silos store wheat until it is milled into flour. Food processing is a leading industry in the state.

Other food-processing activities in Idaho include beet-sugar refining, canning and freezing fruits and vegetables, meat packing, dairying, poultry processing, and making wheat flour and flour products.

The production of chemicals is Idaho's second largest manufacturing industry. Chemicals used in agriculture and other various industries are produced throughout the state.

The third-ranking manufacturing industry in Idaho is the production of electrical machinery—mainly computers and computer-related products. The area around Boise, in southwestern Idaho, is home to nearly half of the state's population. Many high-tech companies have moved there to take advantage of the high quality of life, clean air, and inexpensive hydroelectric power. Hewlett-Packard, for one, has built a large computer factory in Boise. Idaho factories also produce farm machinery and printed materials.

Lumber and wood products are another important area of manufacturing. About forty percent of the state is forested. The majority of these forests contain various kinds of evergreens. Most of Idaho's timber grows in the northern part of the state. Lewiston, which is in the panhandle in the north, has one of the largest sawmills in the world. Boise-Cascade, one of the world's largest paper and wood-product companies, is headquartered in Boise.

As in nearly every state today, service industries are very important to Idaho's economy. Service industries are those in which workers do not make an actual product. Rather, they may work at retail stores, hospitals, restaurants, banks, or hotels. The most important group

Lumbering is a major industry, since nearly forty percent of Idaho is covered with forests.

of service industries in Idaho are finance, real estate, and insurance. Retail trade and wholesale trade rank second. Retail businesses sell things to the public, while wholesale businesses sell goods to the retail businesses. Taken all together, Idaho's service industries contribute about two-thirds of its Gross State Product.

Sun Valley is best known as a ski resort, but it also provides traditional summer tourist activities such as golf, tennis, fishing, and biking.

Mining is a far less important industry today than it once was. Mining brings in only about one percent of the gross state product. Nevertheless Idaho still boasts of the largest silver mine in the country, Sunshine Mine in Shoshone County. Millions of dollars' worth of copper, gold, lead, and other metals are also mined. Idaho produces a great deal of phosphate rock, which is used in making fertilizer. Idaho received its nickname—the Gem State—from the wealth of gemstones that can be found in the mountains.

One industry that has become increasingly important to Idaho is tourism. The beauty of its wilderness and vacation areas, such as Sun Valley, have brought thousands of tourists into the state. Idaho has more than two thousand lakes and fifty mountain peaks of ten thousand feet or higher, many of them in protected forests and wilderness areas.

The people of Idaho have built a strong economy while protecting their natural resources. The rewards are enduring: an abundance of clean air and water and a promise of the same for their children.

31

The Potato Through History

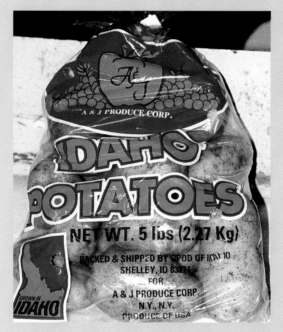

The light-brown Idaho potatoes are famous nationwide. Their proper name is "Russet Burbank."

Say "Idaho" to someone and you'll probably soon find yourself in a conversation about potatoes. The two are as identifiable as movies and Hollywood or pyramids and Egypt. Therefore, it may come as a surprise that the potato is not native to Idaho; it came from South America. But its route to Idaho took it through most of Europe first.

Pedro Cieza de León led a group of Spanish explorers through the Andes Mountains in Peru and Bolivia during the early 1500s. They had never seen a potato before. The Spanish were amazed that a Native American group called the Inca were digging potatoes out of the ground and using them as food. The potatoes Cieza de León saw didn't look much like our potatoes of today. They were small—not much larger than a peanut. But they were unquestionably the same vegetable as the one we eat.

The Spanish explorers were always looking for new sources of food, so they tried the *batatas,* the Incan name for potatoes. They also provisioned their ships with them for the long journey home. They stayed edible far longer than most other vegetables or fruits.

Potatoes are not grown from seeds. They grow on plants that develop from tubers that sprout from the buds, or "eyes," on a seed potato. Bury a potato containing at least one bud, and in a couple of months, there will be a new potato plant. The Spanish explorers learned this from watching the Incas. They used the potatoes they didn't eat on the way home to grow new plants in Spain.

Gradually the popularity of the potato spread across Europe. At first potatoes were considered fancy food; they were expensive and were eaten only by the very rich. But soon everyone became aware of their many advantages. For example, potatoes are easy to grow, and they store well. They are nourishing, filling, and they can be cooked in a variety of ways. Best of all, potatoes will grow in conditions harsh enough to kill many other crops.

Not everyone thought that potatoes were such a good thing. Some early European scientists believed potatoes were poisonous or caused leprosy. Some clergymen even preached sermons against potato-eating as sinful.

Eventually European rulers began to encourage farmers to grow potatoes. In 1651 Frederick William I of Prussia even ruled that anyone refusing to grow and eat potatoes would have his nose and ears cut off! Not surprisingly within ten years potatoes were a staple of the Prussian diet.

Meanwhile the potato had traveled back across the Atlantic. In the early 1600s the English brought

These potatoes are on their way to be peeled, cut up, and canned.

This photograph from the late 1800s shows a woman holding a single potato plant, with its yield of potatoes at her feet.

Hampshire. By 1750 potatoes were an established crop at both ends of the American colonies.

Today, potatoes are grown in many countries and throughout the continental United States. The leading potato-growing nations, in order, are Russia, Poland, and the United States. In the United States, the largest potato producers are Idaho, Washington, Wisconsin, Ohio, and Connecticut. As potato popularity spread throughout the world, different varieties developed. More were created by scientists for size, taste, or some other quality. Today, there are hundreds of potato varieties. However, sweet potatoes and yams are not among them. These vegetables are not related to the potato even though they resemble them somewhat, and they grow in the ground.

Settlers took potatoes with them on their journeys to the West. When the settlers—and their potatoes—reached Idaho in the mid-1800s, the vegetable had found a perfect home. The mountain fields of Idaho are very much like the mountainous home of the Inca. The days are warm, but the

potatoes to the island of Bermuda. From there they were part of a shipment of food to the Jamestown, Virginia, colony in 1621. Then, in the early 1700s, Irish immigrants brought potatoes with them to New

nights are cool. The soil is light and slightly sandy. Rainfall is adequate but not excessive.

Early in this century, Idaho potatoes were well known for their high quality and good taste. Since then the Idaho Potato Commission has used advertising to make sure we never forget that Idaho is the nation's leading potato-growing state.

In the 1950s, however, the popularity of the potato was fading. People were turning to fast, convenient foods, instead. Fewer people regularly had time to cook something that took an hour to boil or bake. Then, an Idaho potato farmer named J. R. Simplot found a way to process potatoes into a fast-cooking food. He developed the first commercially viable frozen french fries. Today, more than half of all the potatoes grown in Idaho are sold as processed products of some kind. It just shows what can be done with a little creativity and a vegetable as easily adaptable as the potato.

These potatoes are being harvested by a mechanical picking machine.

The average person in the United States eats 87 pounds a year of processed potatoes, such as french fries and potato chips.

Living Lightly on the Land

Many cultures see nature as a force to be conquered, but in Idaho nature is a force to be respected. Idahoans have always managed to make nature a vital part of their culture and traditions.

Native Americans have lived in Idaho for at least ten thousand years. The Nez Perce are one of the largest and oldest Native American groups in central Idaho. The Nez Perce were animists, which means that they believed that all things—animals, plants, rocks, stars, and natural forces, such as wind and rain—had spirits. The Shoshone, in southern Idaho, believed that animals created the world and established social customs for humans to follow.

Because of their beliefs, the Nez Perce and the Shoshone treated the land with great respect. For example, when the Nez Perce killed a deer, they were careful to use every part of it. The hide was used for clothing, the bones were used to make needles, and the meat was eaten or dried for winter.

A large part of Idaho remains as natural as it was when Native Americans were its only human inhabitants.

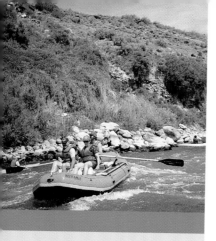

Idaho has many miles of whitewater rivers.

Nez Perce and Shoshone children in their early teens traditionally went on what is called a "vision quest." They spent a period of time alone in the hope that they would have a vision. Spending time alone in nature was a spiritual tradition that helped young people to determine their future roles in life.

Today, people from many other parts of the world live in Idaho, and only a small percentage of Idaho's population is Native American. But the people of Idaho are still outdoor people. Much of Idaho is wilderness. On average Idaho has 12 residents for every square mile of land. Idaho has a larger area of protected wilderness than any state except Alaska. Idaho contains fifteen large national forests, twenty-two state parks, and three huge wilderness areas.

These wild areas are what drew Nobel Prize winning author Ernest Hemingway to Idaho in 1939, at the age of forty. Like many Idahoans, Hemingway loved hunting and fishing and the strong beauty of the landscape. He did much of the work on one of his greatest novels, *For Whom the Bell Tolls*, at the Sun Valley Lodge.

Shoshone Falls on the Snake River in southern Idaho is fifty feet higher than Niagara Falls.

He eventually bought a home in Ketchum, near Sun Valley. Hemingway died in Idaho in 1961 and is buried in the Ketchum cemetery.

Even if you don't like hunting and fishing, there are plenty of things to do outdoors in Idaho. Many of Idaho's cities host outdoor music festivals. The Idaho Shakespeare Festival also takes place outside during the summer. The Boise River Festival and Snake River Stampede are also popular summer events. Rexburg hosts an outdoor international folk dance festival.

Idaho also hosts several rodeos and county fairs, such as the Caldwell Night Rodeo and the Twin Falls County Fair and Rodeo. Teton Valley is home to the Teton Hot Air Balloon Race, and Blackfoot hosts Idaho's World Potato Exposition. Idahoans also love riding the river rapids, hiking, rock climbing, and camping.

People from all over the world come to Idaho to renew their spirits. Residents of this state all seem to share a deep love of nature. As long as Idaho protects its wilderness, it will provide a refuge not only for plants and animals, but for its human population, too.

In 1939 Hemingway did much of the writing for his novel *For Whom the Bell Tolls* at the Sun Valley Lodge.

This man is wearing traditional Nez Perce clothing. There are only about two thousand Nez Perce still living on Idaho's Nez Perce reservation.

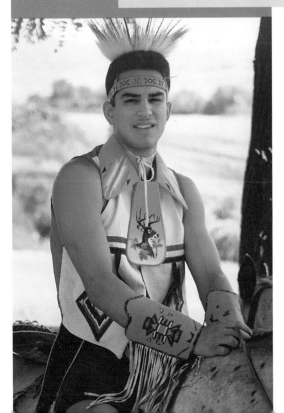

A Mountain Life

Marlin and Susan Kennedy and their son and daughter, Spike and Sammie, live an outdoor life in the Idaho wilderness. It's the kind of life that might seem like paradise to some people.

When their children were small, the Kennedys lived and worked on a ranch in the mountains of northern Idaho. There, near the Snake and Salmon rivers, they lived a primitive life. "We ranched a lot like they did 50 or 75 years ago," Marlin recalls. "Probably the big difference was that we didn't pack our supplies in like they did. But we would only buy our main groceries every six months. The fresh stuff came in on a boat once a week."

The Kennedys didn't have all the conveniences of modern ranching. They didn't herd cattle with airplanes or Jeeps. They did it the old-fashioned way—on horseback. The whole family pitched in and helped.

"Back when Spike was about six and Sammie was four," Marlin says, "they started going out with us. Me and my dogs would stay on one side and keep the cattle together. Susie would be on the other side. Even at that age, the kids knew just where to go. They were probably just as good hands as anybody we could have hired to come in and help us."

At the ranch Spike and Sammie had a very different life from most other children their age. There were no schools anywhere around. So Susan taught them herself at the kitchen table.

The Kennedys chose to live and work on that ranch for a lot of reasons. They liked the freedom. They liked the beauty that surrounded them. And they liked being together. "Our family became very close together out there. In town it seems like part of a family's always going one

Marlin (right, in cowboy hat) has roped a calf and waits for workers to brand the animal.

In the remote regions of Idaho, many ranchers still herd their cattle the traditional way, from horseback with dogs assisting.

Susan Kennedy promotes the family outfitting business at a 1995 sports show.

way and part the other. On the ranch, we could spend more time together. It was good for the kids."

When the children became teenagers, they needed to be around other young people. So, in 1991 the Kennedys sold their cattle and left the remote ranch. For a time they ran a small family-owned business called Hatpoint Outfitters on the Snake River in Hells Canyon, America's deepest gorge. Outfitters are people who guide tourists through wilderness areas. Sometimes they lead teams of hikers or horseback riders. Other outfitters specialize in boat trips or floating over rapids in rubber rafts. In the mountains of northern Idaho, outfitting is a major industry.

The Kennedys, including Spike and Sammie, provided whitewater jet boat trips and horse pack trips in the summer and guide hunting parties in the fall. They are no longer in this business, but they're still outdoors and they're still in the midst of Idaho's wilderness.

Tomorrow's Idaho

The effects of modern technology are just now starting to be felt in Idaho. For the most part, Idaho's air is still clean, and its waters are still clear. There is still plenty of room. Idaho is one of the most sparsely populated states in the country. Pollution and the urban problems that plague many states are minimal. But as more and more people discover this beautiful state, Idaho is challenged to hold onto these valuable assets.

To some extent there have already been reasons for concern. In some Idaho rivers, the fish population has severely fallen off. Part of the problem might come from fertilizing chemicals used in farming that soak into the ground. These chemicals are eventually carried to the rivers. So are waste products from mining. Even ordinary soil, released when land is cultivated or logged, can pollute rocky-bottomed mountain streams and alter fish populations.

Dams that provide cheap, nonpolluting hydro-electric power also harm fish. The dams change the

Boise combines its role as a center for trade and agriculture with respect for the environment. Boise is known as the "City of Trees."

This is a Hewlett-Packard computer factory in Boise. Education is the key to Idaho's future in the high-tech industry, since twenty percent of Idahoans employed by these firms are scientists and engineers.

depth of rivers, their speed, and the water temperature. These changes can kill millions of fish.

Naturally, the people of Idaho do not want to hold up progress. The state government is busy trying to attract more businesses. It points to the clean air, low taxes, and inexpensive electricity as benefits to moving to Idaho. In addition some Idaho residents would like to see increased development of the wild areas. They argue that more mining and logging would mean additional money for the state. Others, who feel the Idaho wilderness is a unique national treasure, want the unspoiled areas to remain protected.

Progress versus protection are issues that will continue to be discussed for many more years in Idaho. Idaho is dependent on its natural beauty to attract new businesses. Some compromises will have to be made. Perhaps more than most states, Idaho needs to find ways to benefit from nature's bounty without destroying it.

Important Historical Events

1805   Meriwether Lewis and William Clark explore the Idaho region.

1809   Canadian explorer David Thompson establishes a fur-trading post at Pend Oreille Lake, near present-day Hope. He also maps the region.

1819   Spain gives up its claim to all of its territory west of the Rocky Mountains, including Idaho.

1834   Fort Hall and Fort Boise are built.

1836   Presbyterian missionaries Henry H. Spalding and his wife, Eliza, establish the Lapwai Mission, near Lewiston.

1843   A provisional government is formed for the Oregon area, including Idaho. The Mission of the Sacred Heart is established by Jesuits.

1848   Congress organizes the Oregon Territory, which includes Idaho.

1855   Mormons build Fort Lemhi.

1858   The Mormons abandon their settlements after Native American raids.

1860   Mormons return to Idaho and start its first permanent settlement at Franklin. Gold is discovered at Orofino Creek.

1862   Gold deposits are found in the Salmon and Boise river areas.

1863   Congress organizes the Idaho Territory.

1864   Montana is made a separate territory. The Idaho Territory capital is moved to Boise.

1877   After more than three months of fighting and retreating, the Nez Perce are forced to surrender to federal troops.

1878   The Bannock, led by chief Buffalo Horn, are massacred by federal troops.

1884   Lead and silver deposits are found in the Coeur d'Alene area.

1890   Idaho becomes the 43rd state.

1892   Miners in the Coeur d'Alene region go on strike.

1905   Former governor Frank Steunenberg is killed. Harry Orchard confesses to the murder, involving three officials of the Western Federation of Miners.

1910   The dam at Salmon Falls Creek is completed.

1936   Sun Valley resort opens.

1951   The National Reactor Testing Station near Idaho Falls produces the first electricity from atomic power.

1962   Pocatello merges with Alameda to become Idaho's second largest city.

1968   The National Wild and Scenic Rivers Act preserves thousands of acres of Idaho wilderness.

1972   A fire at the Sunshine Silver Mine in Shoshone County kills 91 miners.

1976   The Teton Dam bursts, causing the destruction of several farming communities and at least eleven deaths.

1983   The most powerful United States earthquake in 24 years has its epicenter near Challis in central Idaho.

1988   Drought destroys much of Idaho's crops. Forest fires burn three hundred thousand acres of Idaho woodland.

1990   Idaho celebrates one hundred years of statehood.

1993   A five-year drought ends.

The state flag is royal blue with gold fringe. In the center is the state seal; below that is a scroll with the words *State of Idaho.* On the seal a woman holding scales and a spear symbolizes justice, liberty, and equality. A miner and a sheaf of grain stand for Idaho's farming and mineral wealth. An elk's head and a pine tree represent the state's wildlife and forests.

Idaho Almanac

Nickname. The Gem State

Capital. Boise

State Bird. Mountain bluebird

State Flower. Syringa

State Tree. Western white pine

State Motto. *Esto Perpetua* (It Is Perpetual)

State Song. "Here We Have Idaho"

State Abbreviations. Ida. (traditional); ID (postal)

Statehood. July 3, 1890, the 43rd state

Government. Congress: U.S. senators, 2; U.S. representatives, 2. State Legislature: senators, 35; representatives, 70. Counties: 44

Area. 83,574 sq mi (216,456 sq km), 13th in size among the states

Greatest Distances. north/south, 483 mi (778 km); east/west, 316 mi (509 km)

Elevation. Highest: Borah Peak, 12,662 ft (3,859 m). Lowest: 710 ft (216 m)

Population. 1990 Census: 1,011,986 (7.2% increase over 1980), 42nd among the states. Density: 12 persons per sq mi (5 persons per sq km). Distribution: 57% urban, 43% rural. 1980 Census: 944,038

Economy. *Agriculture:* potatoes, wheat, hay, beef cattle, dairy cattle, sheep, barley, sugar beets, fruits and vegetables. *Manufacturing:* processed foods, computers, farm machinery, wood and lumber products, electrical equipment, chemicals, printed materials. *Mining:* phosphate rock, silver, stone, gold

State Seal

State Flower: Syringa

State Bird: Mountain bluebird

Annual Events

★ Lionel Hampton Jazz Festival in Moscow (February)

★ National Circuit Finals Rodeo in Pocatello (March)

★ World Championship Cutter and Chariot Races in Pocatello (March)

★ Cherry Blossom Festival in Emmett (June)

★ National Oldtime Fiddlers Contest and Festival in Weiser (June)

★ Snake River Stampede in Nampa (July)

★ Western Idaho Fair in Boise (August)

★ Eastern Idaho State Fair in Blackfoot (September)

★ Idaho Spud Day in Shelley (September)

★ Lewiston Roundup in Lewiston (September)

★ Lumberjack Days in Orofino (September)

Places to Visit

★ Balanced Rock, near Castleford

★ Cataldo Mission, west of Kellogg

★ City of Rocks, near Oakley

★ Craters of the Moon National Monument

★ Crystal Ice Cave, near American Falls

★ Farragut State Park, on Lake Pend Oreille

★ Hells Canyon National Recreation Area

★ Idaho City in Boise County

★ Lake Coeur d'Alene in Kootenai County

★ Nez Perce National Historical Park, near Lewiston

★ Sawtooth National Recreational Area

★ Shoshone Falls in the Snake River Canyon, near Twin Falls

★ Sun Valley Ski and Resort Area